SEEDS TO THE WIND

Poems,
Songs,
Meditations

Published by Whatever Publishing
PO Box 3073, Berkeley CA 94703

Library of Congress Cataloging in Publication Data

Donicht, Mark.
    Seeds to the wind.

    I. Title.
PS3554.O4698S4   811'.5'4   79-10662
ISBN 0-931432-04-9

Manufactured in the United States of America

The Seeds are cast to the winds
        in the Fall
    And lay still thru the
        Winter's stormy nights

To burst into Life
        with the Spring's shining sun
    And grow to the Summer's
        sundrenched heights

Seeds to the Wind

Mark Allen

Whatever Publishing
Berkeley, California

Contents

Part I
Like a silent new moon...

The Seeds	page 3
Let us connect	13
The Muses Live	15
Gentle Flight	17
Opening for a Reunion	19
Look Within	21
Making Love...	23
A Prayer...	29
Song for a Deva	31
Love is the answer	33
Brother Moth	35
Lenore's Words	37
An old gnarled road	39
Berkeley graffiti	41
Look up into a clear night's sky	43
At the Wheeler's house in Highlands	45
Fantasies visions and dreams	47
What is this	49
Eucalyptus in the storm	51
Forever United	53
In the Midst of the Battle	55
I finally met an old man	57
If I die young	59
Let the Gypsies be reborn!	61
Like a cat	63
I remember the Moonlight	65
As we lay	67
Waves of music	69
A Love Song	71
As above, so below	73
My Daddy was a young man once	75
Ah, but she's only	77
Ode to a Lady	79
A little kid	81
Once upon a time	83
Spring...	85
Who are you?	87

Part II
...At the threshold of morn

Seeds	93
Beyond this plane	95
What is a poem?	97
Within you	99
Waves crash on the showery rocks	101
Invocation	102
A Prayer in a Dream	104
('Sweet Surrender')	
'A Simple Prayer'	107
The Lord has a Temple	109
At the threshold of morn	111
Notes, Credits, Musings...	113

Part I

Like a silent new moon . . .

Let us connect
    Essence to essence
        Tho hundreds or thousands
        of miles apart

Let us unite
    Soul to Soul
        Mind to Mind
            Heart to Heart

The Muses Live

Come sweet Muse
    Bathed in shimmry light
Come sweet spirit
    Of inspiration bright

Let me be your pen
    Let me be your voice
Let me sing your song
    Let me be your choice

Come sweet Muse
    I am empty and stilled
Awaiting your presence
    Waiting to be filled

Oh sweet Muse
    I live for your touch
Surrounded in beauty
    You've blessed us so much!

Gentle Flight

See the light
  Shining bright
   in the night
    Gentle flight
    within

Hear the sound
  All around
    Mystery of being
     Flowing thru

Feel the love
  In your heart
    Inner wonder
     Mystery of life

Touch a star
  It's what you are
    Eternal flowing
     Mystery of Life

You're a wondrous
  Star creation
    A vessel filled
     with Love and Light
     Divine

Opening for a Reunion

Envision your deepest wishes —
Within us are shimmering
forces of creation!

Just clearly imagine
Whatever you wish
Within the depths of our being
is the power of realization!

Imagine anything from your heart
and it will manifest —
A world without fear
An ocean of love!
Just imagine it, and it's ours
Here and now

Imagine that these words
Bless, and purify
your whole being

Let go
& experience
Rebirth
of what is
!

Look Within

Look within
    and you'll find
        every answer you need

Look within
    and you find
        an ever-ripened seed

Watch it grow
    Watch it grow!
        We're but seeds in the
            Earth

Watch it bloom
    Watch it flower
        Every moment is
            Rebirth

Making Love. . .

I remember every lover
    with such sweet feelings
Dream of divine Dakinis
    with such sweet prayer
Every woman is a blessing —
    God's creation
Every body is a miracle
    The mind's revelation

Every moment of love —
    Sweet inspiration!
Every one is divine
    as they open to their depths
Such exquisite ritual
    Sweet meditation
The forces of creation
    unfolding within us
The Kingdom of Heaven
    is truly within us

Remember the myths
    from our deep past heritage
Leda and the Swan
    Europa and the Bull
The form of God appearing
    in a shower of gold
To a woman of exquisite
    divine earthly beauty

'Dakinis' are the angels from the traditions of Tibet and India — they bring teachings and light. Every woman is a Dakini.

In love are all the teachings
    the deep truths of tantra
In love are the forces
    of the Universe on display
For all to see, to catch,
    to understand
And to enjoy the bliss
    of union of the divine

Within every woman —
    The forces of the Moon
Within every man —
    The forces of the Sun
Moon unites with the Sun
    Eclipsing into One
And a new Moon is born
    And we are reborn
        Continually reborn!

Within every woman —
    The forces of the Earth
Within every man —
    The forces of the skies
Earth and sky unite
    And Heaven is here
Totally illumined,
    if we but understand it
Totally blissed
    with vision divine

If the Universe provides
    you with a lover,
Make love! Enjoy!
    Unite with the Divine
And if the Universe shows you
    You're to be alone,
Reflect! Enjoy!
    Unite with the Divine

—for

The greatest blessing of all
    in Love is that
    It's always ever within us
We're man and woman,
    Old and young
The union is ever within us

So
    We don't have to hold on
        to anyone else
    We don't need a lover
        to be in love

    God takes care
        of all of His creatures
    Even alone,
        We're never alone

    Mother Nature takes care
        of all of Her creatures
    Even alone,
        We're always all One

A Prayer. . .

Sweet Angel,
Shakti of my vision,
Tara, the beautiful compassionate one
    You have so many names. . .

Sweet Spirit of the Universe
    who blesses —
    Shining, radiant
        shimmering body —
    Showing that we are beautiful, too

        All creation is a miracle
            Our very existence
                is bliss

        This is your blessing
            This is your love
                Pointing a way
                    into bliss,
                    into light

    We are not these bodies,
        Beautiful & wondrous
            tho they are
        We are pure energy
            Pure light
            Pure love

        This is your teaching
        The teaching the Universe
        Tells itself thru your mouth

        We are all a wondrous
            shimmering, pure
            ocean of love

Song for a Deva

Sweet thoughts of you
   turn into a love song
A melody too
   comes drifting along
Do you know
   what a beauty you are?
You're a flower
      blossoming bright
   With the light
      of a Star!

Sweet, sweet lady
   An angel in thin disguise
Sweet inspiration —
   I can see it in your eyes

I give to you
   the best gift there can be
I give you a mirror
   and now you see
The wonder you are!
   To see is to be free
Look in the mirror now
   Miracles unfold
      in front of thee. . .

Love is the answer
Love is the key
It can open any door
Give us eyes to see
In our heart lies a secret
And it sets us free:

All we need
is Love

All we need
is Love!

"Brother Moth,
    Why
        Do you fly
            Into the light?"

"Brother Human,
    When we leave our bodies,
        We gain new sight
            Of a still brighter, clearer
                Light."

Lenore's words. . .

I am the source
   Prior to anything
I bathe in the sea
   of my existence

   An ocean of swimmers
      & dancers!

Drink of your existence. . .
   — it is endless. . .

   More luxurious
   than anything imaginable

Just see your life
   It is a precious jewel
      Beyond belief

An old gnarled road
  Slashed into a hill
Past an old faded house
  Crumbling and still

    What memories are here
      of lives and loves past
    What dreams were once here
      Tiny and vast

Wild weeds growing everywhere
  Thru cracks in the floor
The people are gone —
  Nature reigns once more

    Distant voices I hear
      of songs long past
    Now sung by the breezes
      Time goes so fast. . .

All our intensity
  Our dreams and our fears
Dissolve in a moment
  As soon as death nears

    The good search for strength
      To stability they ever cling
    The wise flow with change
      Thru life they ever sing

Berkeley graffiti —

In motion,
    be like water
At rest,
    like a mirror

Respond like the echo
    as tho non-existent

Look up into a clear night's sky
When you can see for
    a billion light years

Then you can see
        Infinity
        beyond our smiles and tears

At the Wheeler's house in Highlands —

Ripples in the pond
    Breezes in the trees
Crickets busily playing
        their instruments
    Butterflies and bees. . .

I feel content
    yet unborn
        like a silent New Moon
While Mother Nature
    so sweetly
        is humming her tune . . .

Fantasies, visions, and dreams
  It's all as real
    as it seems. . .

Waking life, time, space,
    and dreams
  It's all as unreal
    as it seems. . .

What is this

Dance of the

Universe?

It is movement. . .

It is stillness. . .

Eucalyptus in the storm —

Such is the song
   of the Universe:

Casting so many seeds

   to the wind

   it doesn't even care. . .

Forever United

See the bright shining smile on her lips
    In her heart she knows and it shows
Feel the love radiate from her being
     As she sings so soft and low
       She sings so soft and low...

The love light is shining so bright from her eyes
     As she sits so peacefully
Eyes like Krishna, eyes like Shiva
    Shining, radiant and free
      Shining radiant and free!

There's nothing we ever have to say to each other
    All was said at our first glance
A smile, a touch and we're one flowing river
    All life is a dance
      All life is a dance!

A river of love ever flows between us
    Wander where we will we never part
Connection so much deeper than physical presence
    Forever united in our heart...
      Forever united in our heart!

In the Midst of the Battle

In the midst of the battle
    I stopped — I felt so strange
A feeling was growing deep in my heart
    Something's about to change
        Something's about to change...

I opened my eyes and I saw you
    In a way so clear, so new
I took a breath that filled my heart
    And I reached out my hand to you
        And I felt my soul reach out to you

Let's really talk to each other
    And say what we really want to say
All I want is to love you
    To love you in my way
        Let's help each other find a way
            We'll help each other find a way

I finally met an old man
    With light shining in his eyes
With words of truth flowing
        joyfully from him
    Living in eternity's sunrise

I finally met an old woman
    With the beauty of light and love
Contented, centered, unafraid
    Speaking of the Eagle and the Dove

They were artists, they said
    They were married, they were childless
Wandering the world at their whim
    They'd lived together for 50 years
        And love still shown between them

Two shining white heads
    Free of care, free of fear
        Laughing, enjoying, playing
Writing, creating,
    Drinking beer, eating pizza
        Embracing, walking alone,
            and praying

Bless you, old friends, for you've
        given me much. . .
    Hope and joy and admiration
Life doesn't have to end
        sadly and painfully
    Even death can be jubilation!

If I die young, it will be
        a good thing
To die young and strong
            never knowing the pain
Of age and its sorrows
            of a body growing old

If I die middle aged, it will be
        a good thing
To have tasted life fully
            knowing joy and pain
Of life in its fullness
            of life in its rounds

If I die very old it will be
        a good thing
To live full and long
            to see thru the pain
To know life in its depths
            of mystery
            and
                silence. . .

Let the Gypsies be reborn!
   Let them wander again. . .
Thru fields of green grass
   Selling amulets and fennel

Herbs picked from green fields,
   From forests and from deserts
Oils pressed from flowers
   Charms for health and weather

Charms for prosperity
   Charms for your lover
Cures for your sickness
   Cures for your Mother. . .

Healing a blind child!
   It's true! — Working wonders
Throwing cares to the wind
   Living in the moment's wonder

Knowing just when to die
   Being strong til that moment
Tying up all affairs
   Calmly awaiting the moment

When you're free at last
   Of this physical body
Sailing into Eternity
   Sailing into new Life

Like a cat, he walks
at night. . .

Moving thru lamplit
streets. . .

Moving in an air of
Silence

I remember the Moonlight
    Dancing on the ocean
The sound of the surf
    Mirrored in our bodies
The touch of your hand
    Lightly on mine. . .

I remember your eyes
    Shining in the night
Clear jewels of light
    Bright as a star
Glowing and streaming
        With golden light wonder. . .

I remember your body
    So warm, so close
So lovely in the night
    With its own shining sweet light
Flowing together
    Perfectly with mine. . .

    Memories I cherish
        Dancing on the wind
    Memories that unite me
        Ever with you. . .

As we lay
	so closely entwined

We are flying together
	thru infinite space

In silence,
	shimmering, light

Blessed by love —
	Creation's grace

Waves of music,
　　Waves of bliss

Waves of music,
　　Waves of bliss

What is Music?
　　Ecstasy's kiss!

A Love Song

You are my love
　In you I see
My reflection
　Bright and free

And so I crown you
　And place you above me
You gave me a blessing
　When you said
　　you loved me

As above, so below

Galaxies in our fingertips!

Whirling around

Universes in our body

Wonder beyond words...

My Daddy was a young man once —
    And not so long ago —
Roaming thru the fields
        of the mountains
    Wondering what to do. . .

My Mother was a young girl once —
    And not so long ago —
Watching wheat and corn and flax
        grow green
    Feeling the Full Moon,
        filled with dreams. . .

At their first sight they knew
    Their dreams were united
At their first look they saw
    Deep familiar ancient friends

And their love stirred the heart
    of the joyous Universe,
Shining. . . vast. . .
    Love without end

Ah, but she's only
        fourteen years old
     With so many things to do

Ah, and she's only
        fourteen years old
     With growing
        & loving
           & changing
              & leaving
                 & sunshine
                    & rain
                       to go thru

Ode to a Lady

Magic moments
   A treasure I cherish
Your command to man
   Love or perish

    The Divine is the good within you
      Only now can I see
    The Divine is the good within us
      This is our magic key

Many forms you have
   Earth born and spirit born
Sacred and sensual
   Evening and morn

    The Divine is the God within you
      Open your eyes, and you see
    The Divine is the God within us
      This in Truth is our Magic Key

A little kid
    just does her thing
She doesn't stop
    to wonder why

There's far more wisdom
    in the play of a child
Than at first
    may meet the eye. . .

Once upon a time,
   not so long ago,
      a young man sat
         on a red motorcycle
            with a road runner decal

And he stopped for a moment, in the heart of the city. . .

And he looked at a Safeway parking lot in Berkeley
Filled with little black kids playing with Kentucky Fried
   Chicken boxes, and
foxy black ladies in clinging tight pants revealing exquisite
   asses, and
old people moving slowly along, alone with their shopping
   bags on wheels, and
young intense people gathering in groups and flirting with
   each other, and
students being very busy, and
panhandlers being very relaxed. . .

And he saw a vision of harmony on this planet —
   outspread before him
      like a medieval painting

               A vision
            of the wonder
             of what is

Spring. . .

The fruitful earth
   Springs forth again
Ever-dying/ever-renewing

Let's live our lives
   like the little green
      leaves
Bursting forth with joy,
   Never fearing
     for a moment
        the Winter to come

When they fall,
   faded and worn,
Only to be born again
      forever

As the fruitful earth
   Springs forth again. . .

Who are you?
  Can you see
    Thou art that —
      An ever-growing tree

What are you?
  Can you hear
    Thou art that —
      An ocean deep and clear

Who are you?
  Can you feel
    Thou art that —
      All that is real

What are you?
  Can you know
    Thou art that —
      Light's eternal glow. . .

Part II

At the threshold of morn

Seeds

Once I saw a vision bright!
   Its shining light foretold
The dawning of a new bright age
   As sang the sage of old

But then. . . my vision was forgot
   In harsher light of day
Forgotten were the sage's words
   Forgotten secrets of children's play

But now, new signs, new stars, new words
   A dawning vision brightly shown
Within the fruits of this Age of Destruction
   The seeds of a New Age are found

       Seeds of bliss!
       Seeds of joy
     Seeds of long-forgotten
         wonder
       Seeds of light
       Seeds of love
     That time can ne'er
      Rend asunder

In our dreams have secrets been revealed
   Which our last dark age had concealed
But it's still a secret —
   only for those who see:
   Freedom is won only by those
     who can dream they're free

Can you see it, sweet sister?
   Can you hear it, dear brother?
It's writ large in signs
   for all to see

     So many don't look. . .
     So many pass by. . .
   And they never really taste
       being free

Beyond this plane
    is an astral plane
Where what we imagine
    takes form

Beyond what we see
    is an energy
Glowing, life giving
    and warm

— In your mind's eye —
Place a pyramid of golden
    light
    over your head...

Let it shower forth bliss...
    Let it renew you...
Into a golden region
    you are led

What is a poem?
  Words in my mind. . .
  Words I can speak to you

What is a word?
  The seed of creation
  The force of God coming thru

Speak to the heavens
  The things you desire
Image them clearly
  In your mind's inner eye

These words set in motion
  The miracle of creation
It will all come to pass
    By and by. . .

Ask and you shall receive
  See and you will find
Knock and the door will be
      opened for you
Into the wonder of the
      Creative Mind

Within you
    is all the beauty of Shakespeare
Within you
    is the depth of William Blake
Within you
    is the joy of Whitman and Ginsberg
Within you
    are the Dawn Visions of Daniel Moore

Within you
    is the strength and light of Moses
Within you
    is the light and life of Christ
Within you
    is the mind and light of Buddha
Within you
    is the light and magic of Padma Sambhava

Within you
    are Brahma, Vishnu, Shiva
Within you
    is the dance of life
Within you
    is the Universe unfolding
Within you
    is
                infinity

Waves crash on the showery rocks
     Children dance on the sand
Wild movement, freedom, bliss
     Children dance on the sand

From out of the waves, spirits appear!
     Shining, silvery spirits of the sea
Called forth by the children's dancing joy
     Summoned forth by a child's free energy

          Dance, dance! Children dance
               Spread your astral wings
          Dance, dance, people dance
               Hear your spirit as it sings

The spirits tell the children wondrous words
     Of the magic beings they really are
Every child is enflamed with magic power
     Every child is a showering star!

The children see and hear, and know
     Strange and wondrous tho it seems
None of the children will ever forget
     Seeing their visions
          and dreaming their dreams

Invocation

Practice, practice the names very slow
   Call the Mage and the Wise Ones — Come!
Summon forth their Spirit by the power of their names
   They will come . . . they will come!

Call upon any spirit you resonate with
   Call upon any name that appeals to you
Jesus or Buddha or Shiva or Krishna
   or Mary or Spirit Guide or any you wish to do. . .

      Call your own name —
        Call it to the winds!
      See your own light,
        Your own higher self
      Your name — a connection
        with the whole Macrocosm
      Your name — a translation
          of
          I AM THAT I AM

I am! a person with my own name
  Known to my friends in this life on Earth

I am that! a connection with the whole Macrocosm
  Known for all time in Eternal Re-birth

I am that I am!
  The whole and the part
  Every level of the divine tree!

I am that I am!
  The whole Universe is mirrored,
  Reflected in you,
    reflected in me!

      I am that I am!
        A mantra of power
      I am that I am!
        Of substance divine
      I am that I am!
        Eternal life force
      I am that I am!
        Quintessential design!

A Prayer in a Dream
('Sweet Surrender')

Teach me, O teach me
    Sweet surrender
Teach me, O teach me
    Now
Show me, O show me
    Blessed Inner Wonder
Show me, O show me how

I pray to deeply understand
    Sweet surrender
May I have the wisdom
    Now
To know what things can change,
    and have the strength to change them,
And to see what things cannot change,
    and let them flow

May I never forget
    Sweet surrender
May I learn, really learn
    to love it all!
There's nothing to reject,
    there is beauty and wonder
In each eternal moment
    here and now

May I forever know
    Sweet surrender
May I learn what it means
    to be free, to be free!
May I live in love,
    may I remember
Everything has its beauty
    tho not everyone can see

Blessed are the beggars
          wandering in the streets
Blessed are the sick and poor
          yearning to breathe free
Blessed are the young and old —
          all brothers and sisters
Blessed is all humanity —
          all life, all humanity!

Blessed is our sadness
          blessed is our joy
Blessed is our longing
          and our pain, our pain!
Blessed is our discontent,
          blessed is our bliss
That which falls,
          and that which rises again

Blessed is the seed,
          the force of creation
Blessed the destruction
          of all created things
Blessed is our separateness —
          for we're divided for love's sake
In order to be
          united again

I pray to deeply realize
          Sweet Surrender
I pray to have the heart
          and eyes to see, to see
That good and bad,
          and right and wrong,
          and pain and bliss, and all
Are all branches of
          the very same tree
They're all one in their
          real identity
They're all One in
          Truth's Infinity

'A Simple Prayer'

Lord, make me an instrument
   of your peace
Where there is hatred
   Let me sow love
   Where there is injury
     Let me sow pardon
   Where there is doubt
     Let me sow faith
   Where there is despair
     Let me sow hope
   Where there is darkness,
       light!
   Where there is sadness,
       joy!

O Divine Master,
  Grant that I may not so much seek
    to be consoled, as to console
    to be understood, as to understand
    to be loved, as to love

        for

It is in giving that we receive
It is in pardoning that we are pardoned
It is in dying that we are reborn
        to Eternal life

— St. Francis

The Lord has a Temple
In silence it dwells
In peace it is found
In light it is surrounded

With eyes closed, it is seen
With inner light it is shown
Thru prayer is a key
Thru prayer it is known

Ask and you shall receive!
Seek and you will find
Knock and the door
will be opened
unto you

Into light for all
Humankind
Light and love
for all kinds of life

At the threshold of morn

Wherever we wander,
   I will call you my friend
No distance between us —
   Nothing to defend
Break all barriers down —
   We have bridges to mend
And a love to lighten
     our laughter
And a love to grow
     everafter

Sisters and brothers
   We will call all humankind
Wherever we wander
   Our heartfriends we will find
A new age of light is born,
   An old dark age is dying
With a love that frees us
     from past karma
A new light, a new law,
   a new dharma

Be in peace . . . be in peace
   In our hearts a new age
     is born
And we sing at the threshold
     of morn!

Notes, Credits, Musings...

These poems are seeds cast to the wind.
Who knows where they may land?
Who knows where they may take root?
Who knows where they may flower?

Part I — Like a silent new moon...

Let us connect — I wrote this for a very beautiful being named Kimberly. Like so many poems, what begins as a feeling meant for one person becomes something for all...

The Muses Live — We are in the process of creating a new mythology, and recreating an old one. We create our own reality, so why not create a magical one? There have been many Muses who have come to me in life, both in so-called 'real' life and in so-called 'imaginary' life...

Gentle Flight — During a rehearsal of our band, Reunion, Robert Powell started jamming on a smooth, watery bassline... soon everybody was playing a new song which had burst forth... and suddenly I was singing these words to go with the music.

Opening for a Reunion — Noj (Jon Bernoff) and I wrote this together one night, on a candle-lit paper bag... and it became the spoken introduction to a huge, new age symphonic rock piece which Noj wrote called "Overture"... It's been recorded, but so far never released. I hope it will be soon — it has shades of Beethoven. (Noj, in fact, may someday write Beethoven's 10th Symphony...)

Look Within — This is a song from my "Seeds" album. Like **Gentle Flight**, it leapt forth spontaneously . . .

Making Love — One golden, sunlit late morning, I was making love with my beautiful friend Shakti. Suddenly I heard these words, almost shouting inside my head. I couldn't ignore them for long, and had to keep stopping and writing them down. It took about two wondrous hours to make love and to hear and write the whole poem . . .

A Prayer — I don't know where this one came from. It spilled out after an intense sauna . . .

Song for a Deva — This is a song recorded on the "Eveningsong" album. I wrote it for Kimberly.

Love is the answer — I sat down one day and played this song, complete, with words and music, as if I had known it for a long time . . .

Brother Moth — This was written in a mountain cabin, watching a moth around a flame, asking it a question, and getting an answer.

Lenore's words — Lenore Schuh wrote these words in her notebook one night in meditation . . . she has pages and pages of notes like this . . . incredible stuff . . .

An old gnarled road — This was written in the mountains of North Carolina . . . I walked past an old gnarled road leading up a hill to a deserted house, and I started hearing these words in my head. I sat down on an old tree stump and wrote the words on a scrap of paper.

Berkeley graffiti — Berkeley has great graffiti — an artform I admire, and occasionally participate in. I saw these words neatly written on the wall of the john outside of The Three C's in North Berkeley. There are masters who scribble on bathroom walls . . .

Look up into a clear night's sky — I heard these words in my mind in the mountains of Highlands, North Carolina, one night when I was taking a piss and staring into the stars...

At the Wheeler's house in Highlands — the pond and the trees and the crickets and the bees played this tune to me...

Fantasies, visions, and dreams — a thought which danced across my mind...

Dance of the Universe — another thought, this time in haiku form (17 syllables).

Eucalyptus in the storm — I spent part of a wintry evening storm sitting, lying, under a grove of giant Eucalyptus trees which were dancing in the wind so ecstatically...

Forever United — This is a love song, which the Reunion Band often plays... It was written for Bucky, a very beautiful and high spirit.

In the midst of the battle — This is a song which Shakti and I wrote together, one afternoon, sitting on our porch in Highlands.

I finally met an old man — One day I was sitting in the courtyard outside of La Val's Pizza in Berkeley, when I spotted this wondrous old couple, whose full white hair and radiant auras glowed brightly, even from a distance. It was crowded, and they ended up joining us for beer and pizza. It was a great blessing for me — I know that they were sent to me to show me how beautiful old age can be... to show me that we can go beyond the usual, sad conceptions people often have surrounding old age...

If I die young — My mother loves this poem... It's very special to me, too...

Let the Gypsies be reborn! — I spent awhile living like a gypsy... I pray that they're coming back among us... that psychics and healers and gypsies and yogis and pilgrims and artists of all sorts will come back among the people. We need the balance of the intuitive mind, the mystic awareness, once again. Some of the ideas in this poem came from things I've read about and by gypsies — like the healing of the blind child and knowing just when to die...

Like a cat — I love walking late at night thru the city or country, wherever I am... Words such as these come to mind...

I remember the Moonlight — this is for Gina, and the memory of a night which I'll always cherish...

As we lay — this is for Shakti, inspired by our hours of silent snuggling... close and wordless...

Waves of music — I don't know where this came from at all...

A Love Song — This is a fragment of a sweet, light love song...

As above, so below — This too is a fragment from a song...

My Daddy was a young man once — Ever think of what your parents' love life was like? My folks have a special connection which I've always loved and admired. You still can catch them snuggling in the kitchen and being very affectionate, after over 40 years of marriage... That's so beautiful to me... and they were married at 19, when they were just kids...

Ah, but she's only — This one's for Kimberly, reflecting a relationship which was, is, and always will be a very beautiful thing...

Ode to a Lady — This popped into my head one night in North Carolina. I don't have the faintest idea where it came from or who it's to... so it must be to everybody...

A little kid — Every kid is a genius, a master. We don't have to educate them — just be educated by them.

Once upon a time — I wrote this wordscape, or whatever it is, sitting on a motorcycle in a Safeway parking lot, relaxing, musing, watching all the activity . . . such is the stuff of life . . .

Spring — These words leapt to mind one Spring as the world leapt to life . . .

Who are you? — I scribbled these words one morning still half asleep sitting in a coffee shop (Sayat Nova) in North Berkeley . . .

Part II — At the threshold of morn

Seeds — This is the opening song in my "Seeds" album . . . it chronicles my life, in a way . . .

Beyond this plane — jottings upon the moon late one night . . . More and more I have come to believe in and encourage the blessings and insights available in meditation and dreams and imaginings and daydreams . . . more and more I've come to value the time I have spent flat on my back watching the clouds go by . . .

What is a poem? — good question.

Within you — this is something else that slipped out when I wasn't thinking about anything in particular, sitting in a coffee shop, staring out a window . . .

Waves crash on the showery rocks — This poem is for every child on the planet . . .

Invocation — These words spilled out very quickly very early one morning... I awoke from a meditation — or was it a dream — and these words were still hanging around, reminiscent of the dream, catching just a shred of it...

A Prayer in a Dream — Late one night I awoke, with the memory of this strange, haunting song still being sung in my mind... A voice said 'write it down!' I said, I'm too tired, I'll do it in the morning. The voice said, quite forcefully, 'do it now — you'll forget it in the morning!' So I sleepily and sloppily wrote the words down. Then I went back to sleep. Then I dreamed a second verse, with the same melody and music. I scribbled that down too. Then a third verse tumbled forth. Then a fourth. And so on, thru the night, until I had eight verses. Finally the song was finished. In the morning, I barely remembered that I had written something. I read the words, and was amazed...

> In my dreams have secrets been revealed...

I've recorded the song in its entirety on "Seeds"...

'A Simple Prayer' — This was written by St. Francis, and it's worth reading over a few thousand times. It was Danny Campbell — our artist — who taught me about St. Francis...

The Lord has a Temple — it's true.

At the threshold of morn — This is recorded on the "Seeds" album, just before the Finale... I wrote the words very quickly one afternoon just as I awoke from a nap... It must be true:

> A new age of light is born,
>   An old dark age is dying
> With a love that frees us
>   from past karma
> A new light, a new law,
>   a new dharma!

Be in peace...

ABOUT THE AUTHOR

Mark Allen is an author, composer, musician, and teacher in the San Francisco Bay Area. His book **Chrysalis — A journey into the new spiritual America** chronicles the last ten years of his life. His other books are **Reunion: Tools for Transformation** (with Shakti Gawain) and **Astrology in the New Age: An Intuitive Approach.** His albums, "Seeds" and "Eveningsong", are put out under his own label, Rising Sun Records. He is presently living and writing and recording in Berkeley, California.

ABOUT THE ARTIST

Danny Campbell is a gifted painter and illustrator who lives in Houston, Texas. He worked in the art department of Vogue Magazine when he was only 18 years old, and he has since proven himself to be a genius artist, illustrator, and puppet maker.